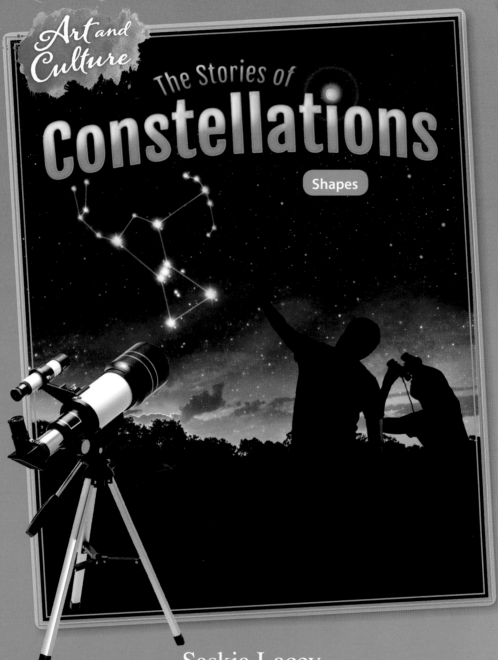

Art and Culture

The Stories of
Constellations

Shapes

Saskia Lacey

Consultants

Michele Ogden, Ed.D
Principal, Irvine Unified School District

Jennifer Robertson, M.A.Ed.
Teacher, Huntington Beach City School District

Publishing Credits

Rachelle Cracchiolo, M.S.Ed., *Publisher*
Conni Medina, M.A.Ed., *Managing Editor*
Dona Herweck Rice, *Series Developer*
Emily R. Smith, M.A.Ed., *Series Developer*
Diana Kenney, M.A.Ed., NBCT, *Content Director*
Stacy Monsman, M.A., *Editor*
Kevin Panter, *Graphic Designer*

Image Credits: p. 8 Mary Evans Picture Library/Alamy Stock Photo; p. 20 Ian Nellist/Alamy Stock Photo; p. 24 (top and bottom) Science Source; p. 25 SPL/Science Source; p. 26 Christophe Lehenaff/Getty Images; all other images from iStock and/or Shutterstock.

Teacher Created Materials

5301 Oceanus Drive
Huntington Beach, CA 92649-1030
http://www.tcmpub.com

ISBN 978-1-4807-5812-4

Table of Contents

Attributes of Ancient Myths

Meet the ancient Greeks. They lived thousands of years ago. Some of history's greatest minds came from early Greece. They invented many things. They built the first theaters. They developed **democracy**. They even built the first showers! Modern society owes much to early Greek culture.

Mythology was very important to the Greeks. They believed in many gods and goddesses. Each had unique **attributes**, or traits. Some gods were known for their strength. Others were known for their wisdom. Still others were praised for their beauty.

The ruins of the Acropolis in Athens are evidence of Greek architecture.

The Parthenon is the ancient temple to Athena.

The city of Athens is named for the Greek goddess Athena.

The Greeks believed that gods and goddesses commanded the forces of nature. They ruled lightning and thunder. They created waves and wind. Each part of nature came from great and unseen powers.

The gods made their home on Mount Olympus. Their ruler was Zeus (zoos), the sky god. Zeus had two brothers, Poseidon (puh-SY-dehn) and Hades (HAY-deez). Poseidon was the god of the seas. Hades was the god of the dead.

In some ways, the three brothers were alike. Each brother was immortal, had great power, and ruled over a realm of Earth. They shared these attributes with one another.

Zeus

Poseidon

6

In other ways, the brothers were different. Zeus was known for his power. Poseidon was thought to be moody. Hades was stern. They each ruled a different level of Earth. Zeus ruled the sky, Poseidon ruled the water, and Hades ruled the underworld. These attributes made them unique.

But attributes are not just used to describe gods and goddesses. They describe many things, such as trees, animals, or even shapes!

Mount Olympus

Hades

Constellations

The Greeks saw shapes in the patterns of stars. They named **constellations** after their familiar myths. This made the stars easier to identify. Today, these stories live on as great shapes in the night sky!

This map shows Greek constellations.

Orion the Hunter

Chances are that you have seen Orion's Belt. It's part of a famous constellation that is named after Orion the Hunter. There are many versions of his birth. Some believe he was the son of Poseidon. Others think he was born from the ground. In any case, the attributes of this star pattern tell us his story. He has a club in one hand. A lion's skin is in the other. These represent his hunting skills. Orion is also wearing a large belt. Its size is a sign of power.

Mythical hero Orion uses his club to battle a lion.

If you look carefully at the constellation, there are lines and angles. There are also shapes called **polygons**. Polygons have certain attributes. They must have at least three straight **sides**, and they must be closed figures.

Orion constellation

Are these shapes polygons? Explain your reasoning for each.

1.

2.

3.

The Orion constellation forms different shapes. What do you notice about the shapes labeled *A* and B? What are their attributes? Both are two-dimensional, closed shapes with straight sides. These are their shared attributes. Because they are closed shapes with straight sides, the shapes can be classified as polygons.

What else can be said about Shapes A and B? They also have four sides. That attribute makes these shapes **quadrilaterals**. A quadrilateral is any polygon with four sides.

Shape C is also a polygon because it is a closed shape with straight lines. But, Shape C only has three sides. So, it is not a quadrilateral like Shapes A and B.

Are these shapes polygons, quadrilaterals, or both?
How do you know?

1.

2.

3.

4.

5.

Can you spot the two
quadrilaterals in Ursa Major?

12

Ursa Major

Another famous constellation is Ursa Major. Part of it is known as the Big Dipper. In Latin, *Ursa Major* means "Greater Bear." The story of Ursa Major has many versions. But they all begin, like many Greek myths, with the powerful Zeus.

The sky god fell in love with Callisto. She was a beautiful nymph. In one version of the story, Zeus's wife finds out about his love for Callisto. She is filled with rage. In her anger, she turns Callisto into a bear.

Another version has Zeus hiding his love for Callisto from his wife. In this story, it is Zeus who turns Callisto into a bear. Later, a hunter sees this bear in the woods. He raises his spear. He is about to attack!

Some versions say Zeus saves the bear. Others say the hunter kills her. In both cases, Zeus places Callisto in the northern sky. Today, she shines brightly as a constellation.

Look closely at the four-sided polygons in Ursa Major. You'll notice that they don't look the same. That is because quadrilaterals do not need to be identical. In fact, they can look very different!

So, what are quadrilaterals? They are not three-sided shapes. Nor are they five-sided. They do not have curved sides. Quadrilaterals are closed shapes with four straight sides.

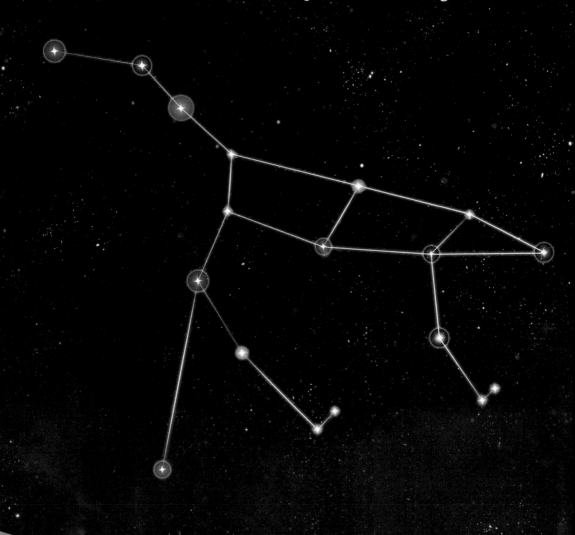

There are many ways to draw four-sided polygons. You could draw them all day and each could still look different. Even so, there are a few types of quadrilaterals that are special. They have been given special names. Some examples are the **square** and **rectangle**.

LET'S EXPLORE MATH

Answer these questions by drawing shapes to prove your reasoning.

1. Is it possible to draw a rectangle that is not a quadrilateral? Why or why not?

2. Is it possible to draw a quadrilateral that is not a rectangle? Why or why not?

Pegasus, the Winged Horse

A great, starry horse flies among the stars. His name is Pegasus. The winged beast is a beloved creature in Greek mythology. Zeus's son was the first to ride Pegasus. Pegasus stands as a symbol of the eternal soul.

In the Pegasus constellation, there is a shape known as the Great Square. But if you look closely at the shape you might ask, is it really a square?

We know that squares have four sides. That is an attribute of all quadrilaterals. But what attribute makes a square unique? For a quadrilateral to also be a square, it must have four equal sides. That means that each side is the same length. Squares also have four **right** angles, or perfect corners.

Use the quadrilaterals to answer the questions.

1. What attributes do a square and rectangle have in common?

2. What attributes of a square and rectangle are different?

The myth of Pegasus, the winged horse, is remembered with statues as well.

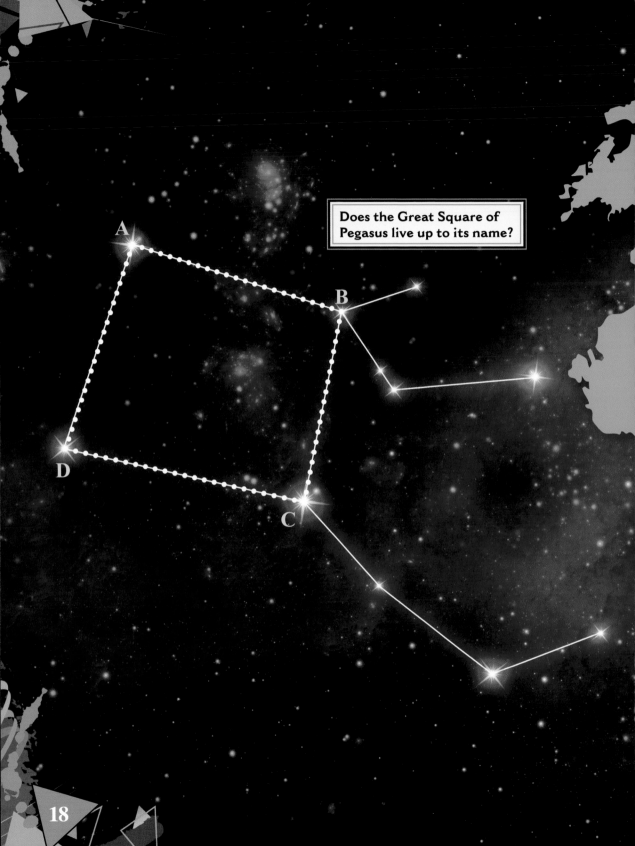

Does the Great Square of Pegasus live up to its name?

The Great Square does not have four right angles. Some of its angles are **obtuse**, or larger than 90 degrees. The angle labeled *B* is an example of an obtuse angle. The Great Square also has **acute** angles. These are angles that are less than 90 degrees. The angle labeled *D* is an example of an acute angle. A true square cannot have obtuse or acute angles; it must have four right angles.

The sides of the Great Square are close to **parallel**, but not exact. A square must have two pairs of precise parallel sides. Finally, a square must also have four equal sides. The sides found in the Great Square are not all the same length. For these reasons, the Great Square is not, in fact, a square. The Great Quadrilateral must not have sounded as catchy, though!

Pegasus's wings and tail can be noticed in its namesake constellation.

Heracles, the Hero

North of Pegasus, another hero can be seen in the stars. He was also a son of Zeus's. The myths of Heracles talk about his strength. He was known for beating many monsters. His wins made him a favorite in the eyes of his mighty father. After Heracles died, Zeus wanted to show how proud he was of his son. So, Zeus placed him in the stars for all to admire.

The Heracles constellation was later named Hercules. The stars connect to form a closed shape with straight sides. This makes it a polygon. The four sides make it a quadrilateral. It also has angles other than right angles. This means that it is not a rectangle or a square. Why? Squares and rectangles must have four right angles.

So, what shape is formed in this constellation? What sets it apart from other four-sided polygons? In this case, the shape's key trait is its one set of parallel sides. A quadrilateral that has one pair of parallel sides is called a **trapezoid**. (Squares and rectangles have two sets of parallel sides.)

Heracles holds up the world.

LET'S EXPLORE MATH

Play "Who am I?" to determine which geometric shape is being described by the clues.

Rectangle   Polygon   Trapezoid   Quadrilateral   Square

1. I have 4 equal sides and 4 right angles.
2. I am any closed shape with 3 or more straight sides.
3. I have 4 right angles. I do not need to have 4 equal sides.
4. I am any polygon with 4 sides.
5. I have 1 pair of parallel sides. I am a quadrilateral.

The constellation of Lyra is found in the northern sky. Vega is its brightest star. In Greek, *Lyra* is "lyre." A lyre is a stringed instrument that is similar to a harp. The ancient Greeks used it to play music.

A Greek hero was known for playing the lyre. His name was Orpheus. He was a musician. Orpheus's singing was enchanted. When he played the lyre, animals danced and trees swayed. His lyre was placed in the heavens to celebrate his legend.

If we look at Lyra, we see a slanted shape. It has four sides. That makes it a quadrilateral. This shape, in particular, is a **parallelogram**. A parallelogram must have two pairs of parallel, opposite sides. Its opposite sides must also be equal in length. It does not need to have four right angles. The shape may have acute and obtuse angles.

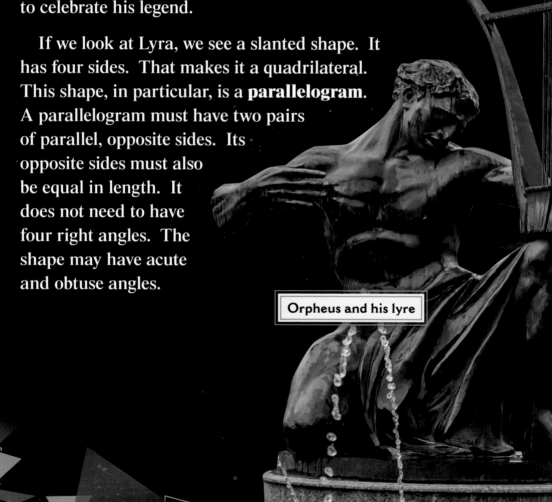

Orpheus and his lyre

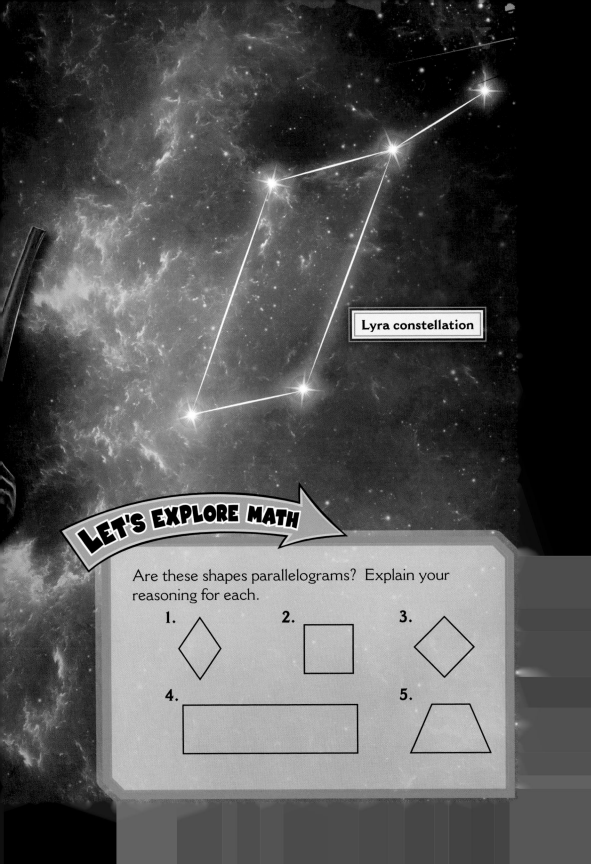

Lyra constellation

LET'S EXPLORE MATH

Are these shapes parallelograms? Explain your reasoning for each.

1.

2.

3.

4.

5.

Maya constellation map

This star map from the 1500s shows ancient Egyptian constellations of the southern sky.

Myth and Meaning

The constellations held meaning for the Greeks. They were also useful. They were not just bright patterns in the sky. They helped farmers keep track of seasons. They gave travelers on land and water clues about where they were.

The Greeks were not alone in studying the sky. Many other people, such as the Egyptians, the Chinese, and the Mayas, found patterns in the stars. They gave the stars their own names. They told their own myths. The star patterns helped them explain everyday events. They were even part of their religions.

In the 16th century, more constellations were named. Explorers from Europe returned home after sailing the seas. They used the stars as guides and named them at the same time.

These groups of people were very different. But, they all had something in common. They wanted to find shapes in the sky and give them meaning.

Chinese celestial sphere

Star Stories

Constellations continue to be studied. People all over the world love trying to find famous star patterns. Scientists use these patterns to find specific stars.

But the search doesn't end there! Stars are still being found today. Sometimes they are named for the person who discovers them. Stars are also named after where they are found in space. Most of these names use numbers and letters. They can have very long names that seem like an endless string of numbers. Or they can have short names, such as Kruger 60 A. The names are not always easy to say. But, they tell scientists important things about each star.

These newly found stars might not have myths attached to them. But, each star has a story of how it was discovered. The lives of those stories will depend on whether they are retold— just like the myths of the Greeks from long ago.

⚙️ Problem Solving

Design a constellation that includes everything on the checklist below. Remember to label each geometric feature. Then, write a myth about the constellation that could be passed on from generation to generation.

Constellation Checklist

⭐ 1 square

⭐ 1 rectangle

⭐ 1 parallelogram

⭐ 1 trapezoid

⭐ 2 polygons of your choice that are not quadrilaterals

⭐ 2 nonpolygons

⭐ 2 acute angles

⭐ 2 obtuse angles

⭐ 2 right angles

Glossary

acute—measuring less than 90 degrees

attributes—qualities or features

constellations—groups of stars that form particular shapes and have been given names

democracy—a form of government in which people choose their leaders by voting

mythology—stories about ancient Greek gods, goddesses, and heroes

nymph—a mythological spirit in the shape of a young woman

obtuse—measuring more than 90 degrees

parallel—the same distance apart and not touching at any point

parallelogram—a quadrilateral with opposite sides parallel and opposite angles equal

polygons—closed, flat shapes that have three or more straight sides and angles

quadrilaterals—polygons with 4 sides and 4 angles

rectangle—a quadrilateral with 4 right angles and opposite sides equal

right—measuring exactly 90 degrees

sides—line segments of polygons

square—a quadrilateral with 4 equal sides and 4 right angles

trapezoid—a quadrilateral with one pair of parallel sides

Index

Answer Key

Let's Explore Math

page 9:

1. No; curved sides
2. Yes; straight sides, closed figure
3. No; not a closed figure

page 11:

1. Polygon: closed shape with straight sides; Not a quadrilateral: more than 4 sides
2. Both, closed shape with 4 straight sides
3. Polygon: closed shape with straight sides; Not a quadrilateral: more than 4 sides
4. Both, closed shape with 4 straight sides
5. Polygon: closed shape with straight sides; Not a quadrilateral: more than 4 sides

page 15:

1. No; all rectangles must be 4-sided polygons.
2. Yes; not all quadrilaterals have equal and parallel opposite sides and 4 right angles.

page 17:

1. 4 sides; opposite sides equal and parallel; 4 right angles
2. All 4 sides of a square must be equal. Not all 4 sides must be equal in a rectangle.

page 21:

1. Square
2. Polygon
3. Rectangle
4. Quadrilateral
5. Trapezoid

page 23:

1. Yes; 4-sided, opposite sides equal and parallel
2. Yes; 4-sided, opposite sides equal and parallel
3. Yes; 4-sided, opposite sides equal and parallel
4. Yes; 4-sided, opposite sides equal and parallel
5. No; 4-sided, but only one pair of parallel sides

Problem Solving

Constellation stories will vary. Constellations must include all of the items on the checklist with geometric features labeled.